Raya's Night Before Christmas
©2022 Alexa Marvel

Contact: alexa@alexamarvel.com

ISBN 978-1-948708-83-8

Printed in the USA

10 9 8 7 6 5 4 3 2 1

For Worldwide Distribution

To my grandchildren who bring me joy!

Hi, my name is Raya! I am 3 years old! I live in South Bend, Indiana with my mom, dad, brother Zane, and my dog Pacey.

FLINT VEHICLE CITY

My grandad and grandmama live in Flint Michigan!

My mom and dad are doctors.
One Christmas, Mom had to work at the hospital.

So, I went with Dad, Zane, and Pacey to spend Christmas with Grandad and Grandmama.

I helped Dad pack the car with gifts for Grandad and Grandmama. Zane put Pacey in his carrier and off we went for the long drive to Michigan.

We drove through town.

It was Christmas Eve and lots of houses were bright with white and colored lights.

Some houses even had reindeer with sleighs and Santas

Dad guided the car onto the freeway tapping his fingers to the Christmas carols playing on the radio. The sun was slowly sinking as we drove from west to east.

Zane turned on his iPad scrolling for his favorite show. I looked out the window hoping to see more brightly lit houses. I guess I must have fallen asleep.

Suddenly - Bump! Thump!
A large, brown reindeer with huge antlers was looking in the car window. I blinked and he was gone with another reindeer right behind him!

Boom! Pop! The car spun around.
Out came the air bags!
Smoke was everywhere!

Dad took off his seat belt and climbed into the back seat to check us out. While he was still examining us, we saw flashing lights coming down the road.

The policeman helped us out of the car. The paramedics checked to see if we had any broken bones even though Dad told them we were okay.

The policeman put all of us, Pacey too, into the back of his cruiser so that we could be warm. It was cold outside.

He called for a tow truck to come and get our car, meanwhile Dad called his sister, Aunt Eloise, to come and pick us up. Dad also called Mom and Grandmama to tell them what happened.

When the policeman flashed his light, we could see that our car was pretty banged up.

Soon, Aunt Eloise and her friend Mike were there to pick us up. We rode in Aunt Eloise's car while Mike took our luggage and gifts in his car.

We finally made it to Grandmama's house late that evening. She opened the door and said, "Is everyone okay?"

I had to tell Grandmama how those reindeer were late for Santa. They were running so fast that they did not look before crossing the road – I mean everyone knows that is what you have to do!

They ran off without even saying they were sorry or
telling us their names! How rude?
I wonder if all of them were Santa's reindeer.

I told Grandmama they had better bring some presents tonight! I talked to Mom on the phone and told her the same thing I told Grandmama.

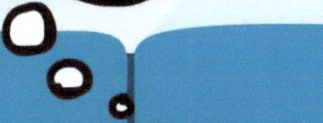

I wonder if those reindeer told Santa what happened. Hmmm!

www.ingramcontent.com/pod-product-compliance
Lightning Source LLC
LaVergne TN
LVHW072101070426
835508LV00002B/219